2 Pupil's Book with Digital Pack

Pippa and Pop

British English

Caroline Nixon & Michael Tomlinson

with Lesley Koustaff & Susan Rivers

CAMBRIDGE
UNIVERSITY PRESS

Map of the book

	VOCABULARY	LANGUAGE	SOUNDS AND LETTERS	LITERACY AND VALUES	NUMBERS	CROSS-CURRICULAR	PROJECT
Introduction Page 4							
1 Hello! Page 6	Review Level 1: characters, clothes, colours, nature, objects, school, toys *black, grey, orange, purple, white*	Review Level 1: *I'm (Kim).* *I'm a (girl).* *I like (books).* *Draw (a butterfly).* *Colour / Paint it (purple).*	Review Level 1 letter sounds: *a, e, i, o, u*	*The colourful chameleon* Celebrate differences	Review numbers: *1 – 10*	Art: Mixing colours	Make a colour wheel
2 My family Page 18	*aunt, uncle, cousin, grandma, grandpa* *funny, old, short, tall, young*	*Who's that?* *He's my (grandpa).* *She's my (grandma).* *She's / He's / I'm (old).* *She isn't / He isn't / I'm not (young).*	Letter sounds: *d, m*	*Anna's baby brother* Be patient	Numbers: *11, 12*	Science: Growing up	Make a family album
3 My home Page 30	*bathroom, bedroom, dining room, kitchen, living room* *cooking, eating, playing, sleeping, washing*	*Where's (Kim / Dan / Dan's mummy)?* *She's / He's in the (kitchen).* *What's she / he doing?* *She's / He's (sleeping).*	Letter sounds: *b, k*	*Hide and seek* Be careful	Numbers: *13, 14*	Maths: Shapes	Make Kim and Dan's apartment
Units 1–3 Review Page 42							
4 My body Page 44	*fingers, head, neck, shoulders, toes* *blonde, curly, long, short, straight (hair)*	*She's / He's / It's got (a neck).* *She's / He's / It's got (long) hair.* *She / He / It hasn't got (short) hair.*	Letter sounds: *t, n*	*Milo's shadow* Be resilient	One less	Science: Shadows	Make a puppet
5 Outdoors Page 56	*cold, hot, rainy, sunny, windy* *boots, jumper, raincoat, sandals, sunglasses*	*What's the weather like?* *It's (hot).* *I'm wearing (a raincoat).*	Letter sounds: *s, h*	*Rainy day fun* Celebrate nature	Numbers: *15, 16*	Science: Rainbows	Make a weather wheel

	VOCABULARY	LANGUAGE	SOUNDS AND LETTERS	LITERACY AND VALUES	NUMBERS	CROSS-CURRICULAR	PROJECT
6 Animals Page 68	chicken, cow, goat, horse, sheep fly, jump, run, swim, walk	It's a (horse). It's got a (long) (neck). A (horse) can / can't (jump).	Letter sounds: c, g	Stubborn goats! Be considerate	More or less?	Social studies: How animals help us	Make a farm animal
Units 4–6 Review Page 80							
7 My favourite food Page 82	burger, lolly, mango, orange, pear bread, cheese, chips, eggs, fish	Can I have (a pear), please? Do you like (fish)? Yes, I do. / No, I don't.	Letter sounds: f, l, p	Pea soup Be helpful	Numbers: 17, 18	Science: Where food comes from	Make food and go shopping
8 My senses Page 94	feel, hear, see, smell, taste bee, grass, leaf, lemon, watermelon	Can you (see) (the rain)? Yes, I can. / No, I can't. What can you (hear)? I can (hear) a (bee).	Letter sounds: j, z	A wonderful day Enjoy the world around you	Recognising patterns	Science: Loud and quiet	Make a senses plate
9 Holidays! Page 106	beach, sea, boats, kites, shells drinking lemonade, eating ice cream, making sandcastles, playing with shells, taking photos	How many (boats) can you see? I can see (four) (boats). I'm (playing with shells).	Letter sounds: v, w, y	You can do it, Sam! Persevere	Numbers: 19, 20	Science: Floating and sinking	Make a beach scene
Units 7–9 Review Page 118							

Welcome back!

BOOKSHOP

Welcome back to *Pippa and Pop*

1 Hello!

▶ 🎧³ **Listen to the song.**

1 Introduction and language review: *Hello. I'm (Kim / Dan / Pop / Pippa). I'm a (girl / boy / mouse). I like (bikes).*

🎧 Listen. 👆 Point. ✏️ Colour.

🎧 5 Listen. 📙 Match. 🗨 Stick. 💬 Say.

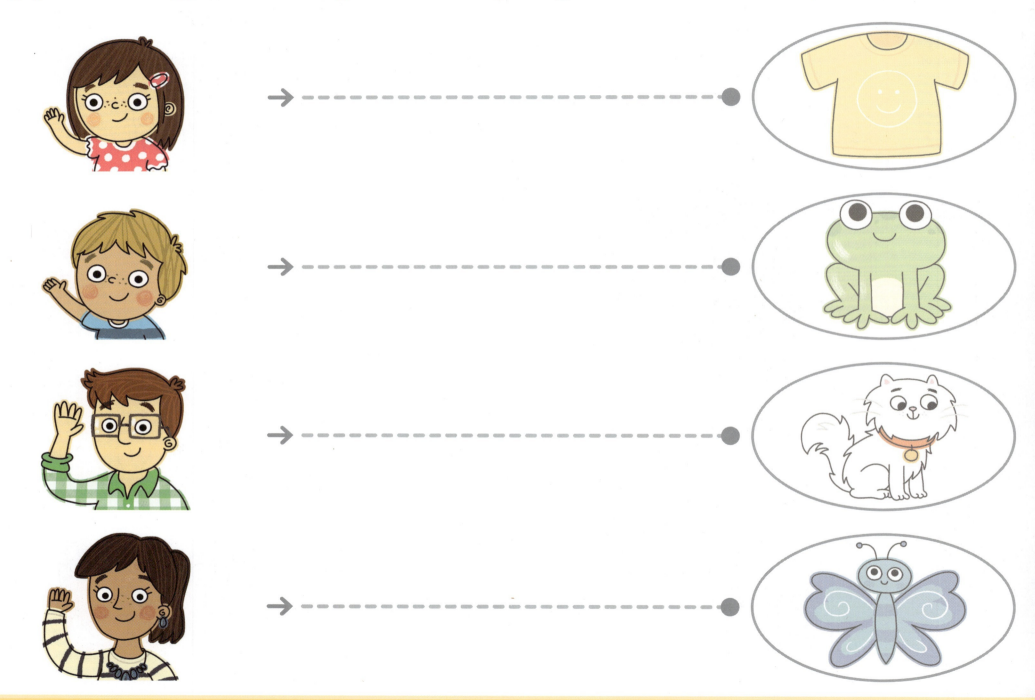

1 **Language review:** *Hello. I'm (Dan / Kim / Sue / Matt). I'm a (girl / boy / woman / man). I like (T-shirts / cats / frogs / butterflies).*

Listen. **Trace.** **Match.** **Say.**

   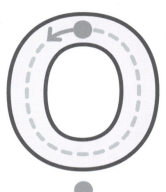 

Listen. The colourful chameleon

5

6

7

8

1 

2 

3 

4 

1   **Language presentation:** *Draw (a butterfly). Colour / Paint it (orange / purple / grey / black / white).*

👁 **Look.** ✋ **Count.** ⭕ **Circle.** ⭕ **Trace.**

1 Review numbers: *1–10*

 **Listen.** **Colour.**

🎧 ¹¹ Listen. ⭕ Circle. 💬 Say.

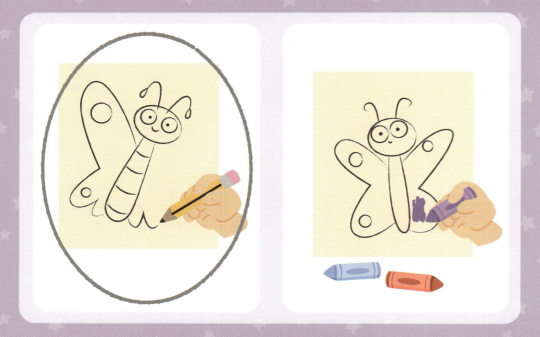

1 *Draw (a butterfly). Colour / Paint it (orange / purple / grey / black / white).*

Look. Make. Say.

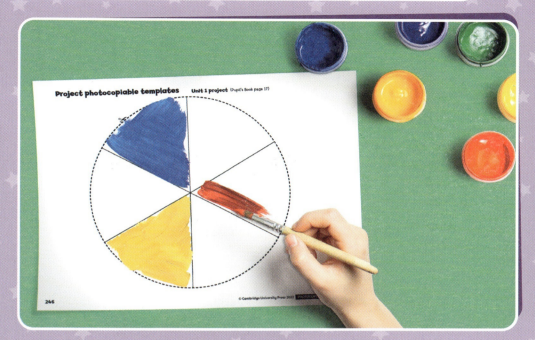

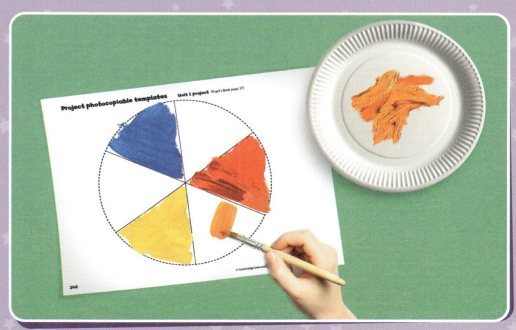

② My family

▶ 🎧12 **Listen to the song.**

② Unit topic introduction: Family

🎧 13 **Listen.** 👆 **Point.** ⭕ **Circle.**

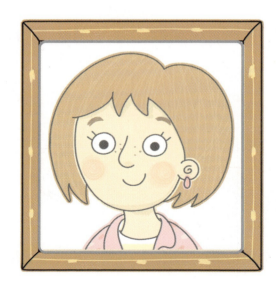

15 🎧 **Listen.** ⭕ **Trace.** ✏️ **Colour.** 💬 **Say.**

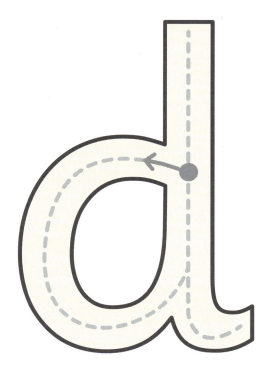

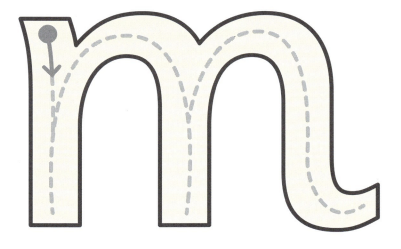

▶ 🎧16 Listen. **Anna's baby brother**

1

2

3

4

2 **Language presentation:** *He's / I'm / She's (tall / short / old / young / funny). He isn't / I'm not / She isn't (tall).*

Listen. ◯ Circle. ♫ Sing.

 **Listen.** **Trace.** **Count.** **Circle.**

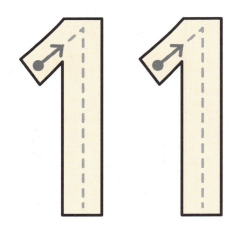  

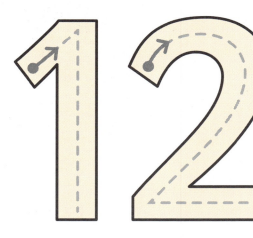  

👁 **Look.** 📙 **Match.**

Look. **Listen.** **Colour.** **Say.**

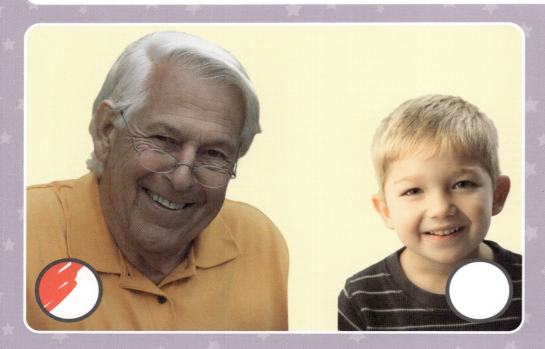

2 *He's / I'm / She's (tall / short / old / young / funny). He isn't / I'm not / She isn't (tall).*

Look. Make. Say.

My family

③ My home

③ Unit topic introduction: Home

🎧²² Listen. 👆 Point. 📙 Match.

🎧 23 Listen. 👆 Point. 🔵 Stick. 🟧 Say.

3 **Language practice:** *Where's Dan / Kim? He's / She's in the (bedroom / bathroom / kitchen / living room / dining room).*

🎧 **24 Listen.** ⭕ **Trace.** ⬭ **Circle.** 🔶 **Say.**

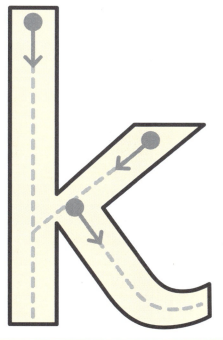

▶ 🎧25 Listen. Hide-and-seek

1

2

3

4

Values

Be careful 3 35

▶️ 🎧 26 Listen. 👆 Point. ⭕ Circle.

1

2

3

4

3 Language presentation: *What's he / she doing? He's / She's (sleeping / cooking / eating / playing / washing).*

▶ 🎧 ²⁷ **Listen.** ➡➡ **Follow.** ✏ **Colour.** 🎵 **Sing.**

🎧 **28** **Listen.** ⭕ **Trace.** ✋ **Count.** ⭕ **Circle.**

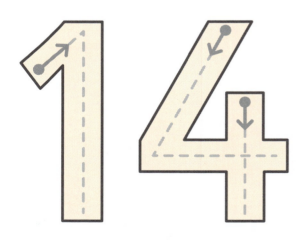

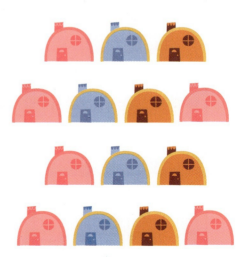

🎧²⁹ Listen. ⭕ Trace. 🟧 Match.

Review

 Listen. **Circle.** **Say.**

3 *What's (Daddy / Mummy / Grandma / Grandpa) doing? He's / She's (sleeping / cooking / eating / playing / washing).*

 👁 **Look.** 🙌 **Make.** 😊 **Play.**

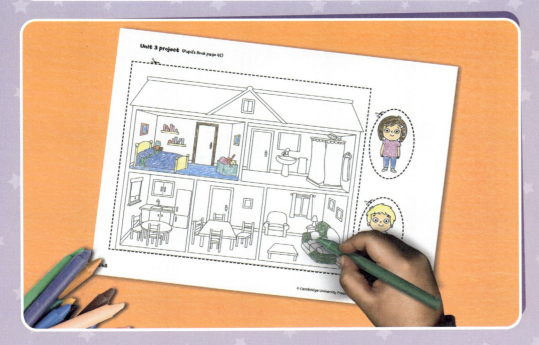

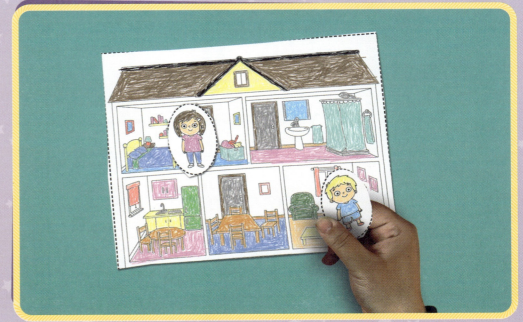

31 Listen. Find. Circle. Say.

👁 Look. ✋ Count. ✏ Colour.

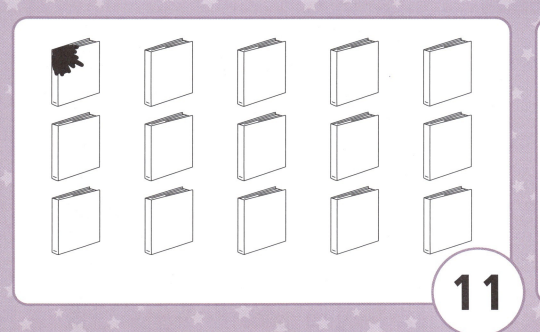

11

12

13

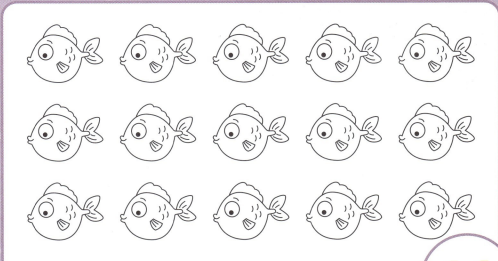

14

4 My body

  Listen to the song.

🎧 33 **Listen.** 👆 **Point.** ⭕ **Circle.**

🎧 34 Listen. ☝ Point. 🔵 Stick. 💬 Say.

4 Language practice: *He's / She's / It's got (a neck / a head / shoulders / toes / fingers).*

35 🎧 **Listen.** ⭕ **Trace.** ✏️ **Colour.** 💬 **Say.**

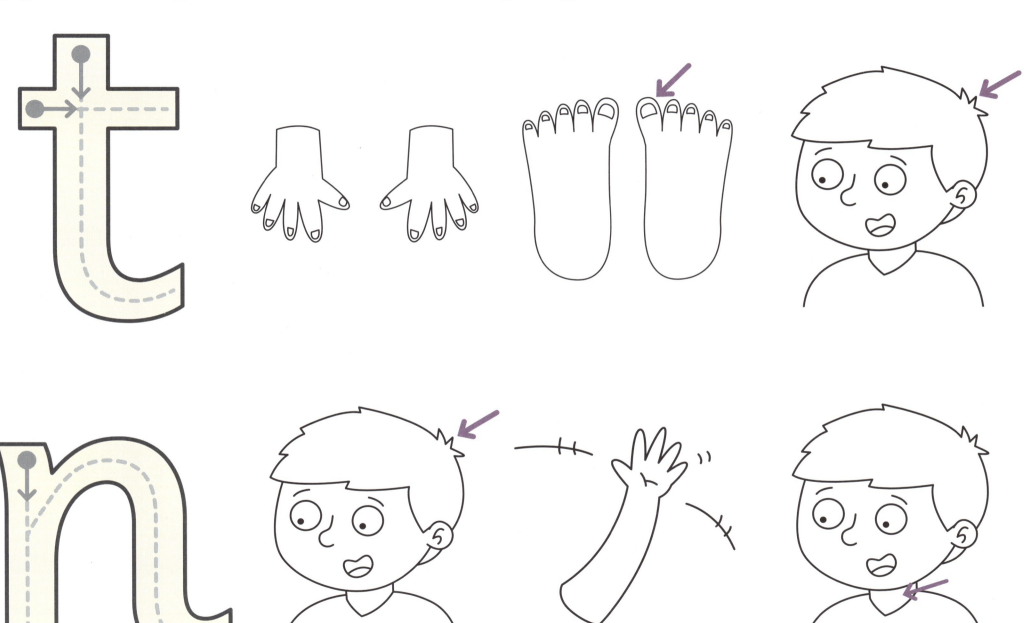

▶ 🎧37 Listen. 👆 Point. ⭕ Circle.

4 **Language presentation:** *He's / She's got (long / short / blonde / straight / curly) hair. He / She hasn't got (long) hair.*

 **Listen.** **Draw.** 🎵 **Sing.**

Numbers

✋ **Count.** ⭕ **Circle.**

👁 Look. 📙 Match.

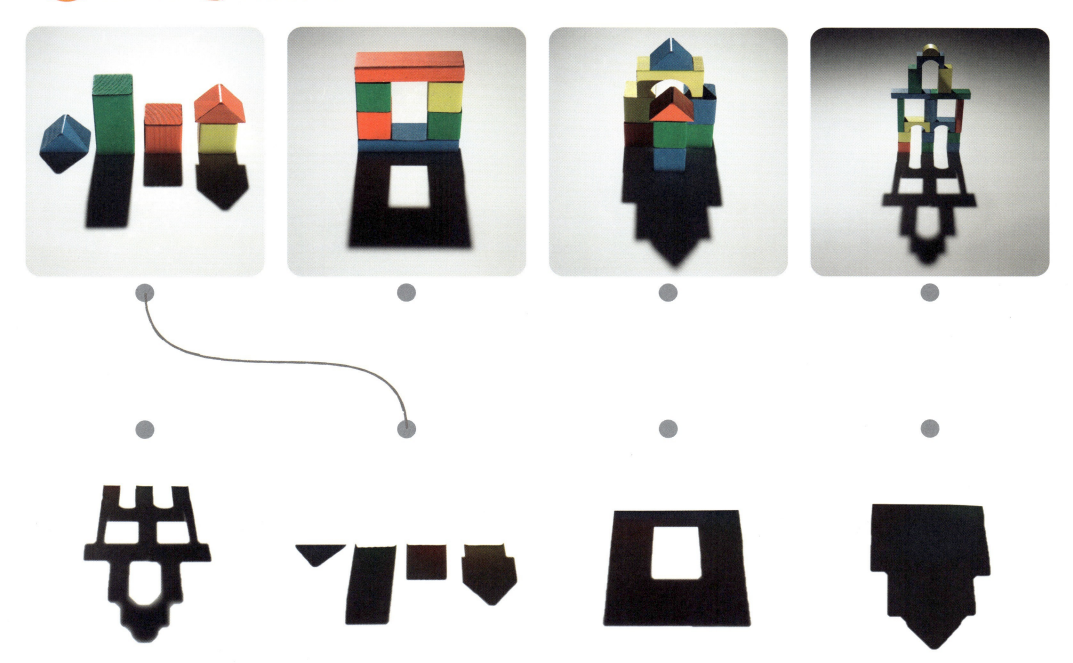

Look. ○ **Circle.** **Say.**

1

2

4 *It's got a (big / small) head. It's got (six / eight) toes. She's got (curly / straight) hair. He's got (small / big) shoulders.*

Look. **Make.** **Say.** **Play.**

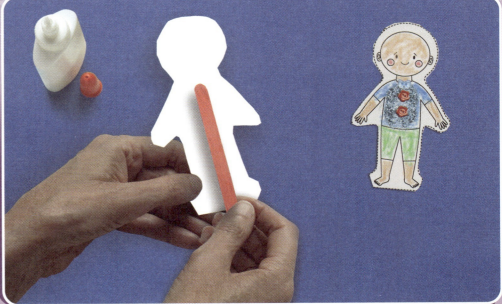

He's / She's got (long / short / blonde / straight / curly) hair. He / She hasn't got (long) hair. 4 55

5 Outdoors

▶ 🎧 39 **Listen to the song.**

5 **Unit topic introduction:** Outdoors

🎧⁴⁰ Listen. 👆 Point. ⭕ Circle.

🎧 41 Listen. ⬭ Stick. ⭕ Trace. 🟧 Say.

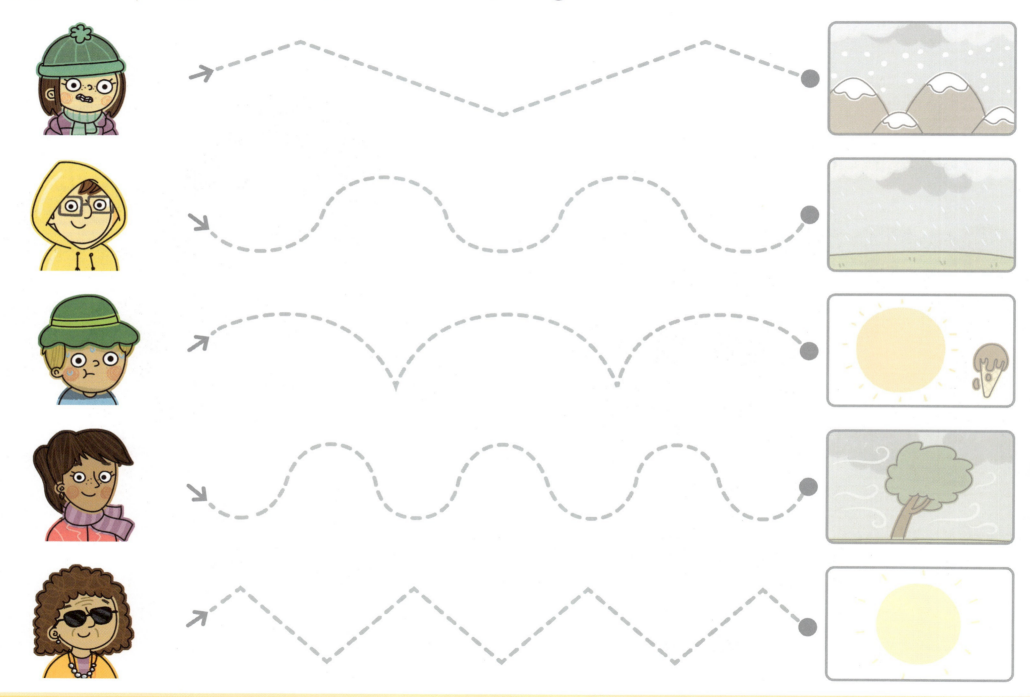

5 Language practice: *What's the weather like? It's (sunny / rainy / windy / hot / cold).*

🎧 42 **Listen.** ⭕ **Trace.** ✏️ **Colour.** 💬 **Say.**

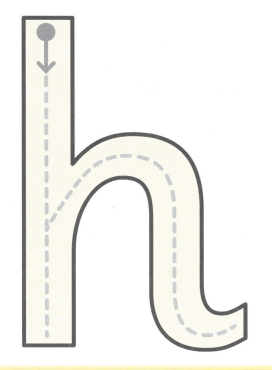

Listen. Rainy day fun

1

2

3

4

Listen. **Point.** 🖊 **Colour.**

5 **Language presentation:** *I'm wearing (a jumper / a raincoat / sandals / sunglasses / boots).*

45 Listen. ○ **Circle.** ♫ **Sing.**

🎧 46 **Listen.** ⭕ **Trace.** ✋ **Count.** ⭕ **Circle.**

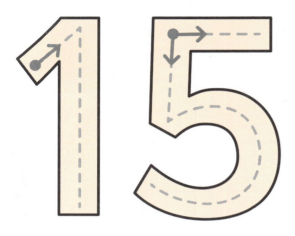

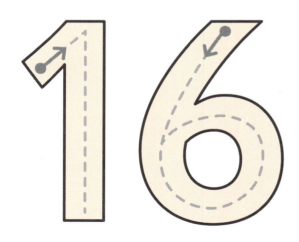

👁 **Look.** ✏ **Colour.** 💬 **Say.**

Look. ✏️ Draw. 💬 Say.

5 *I'm wearing (a jumper / a raincoat / sandals / sunglasses / boots).*

👁 Look. 🙌 Make. 💬 Say.

What's the weather like? It's (sunny / rainy / windy / hot / cold). **5**

 6 Animals

  Listen to the song.

48 Listen. Point. Circle.

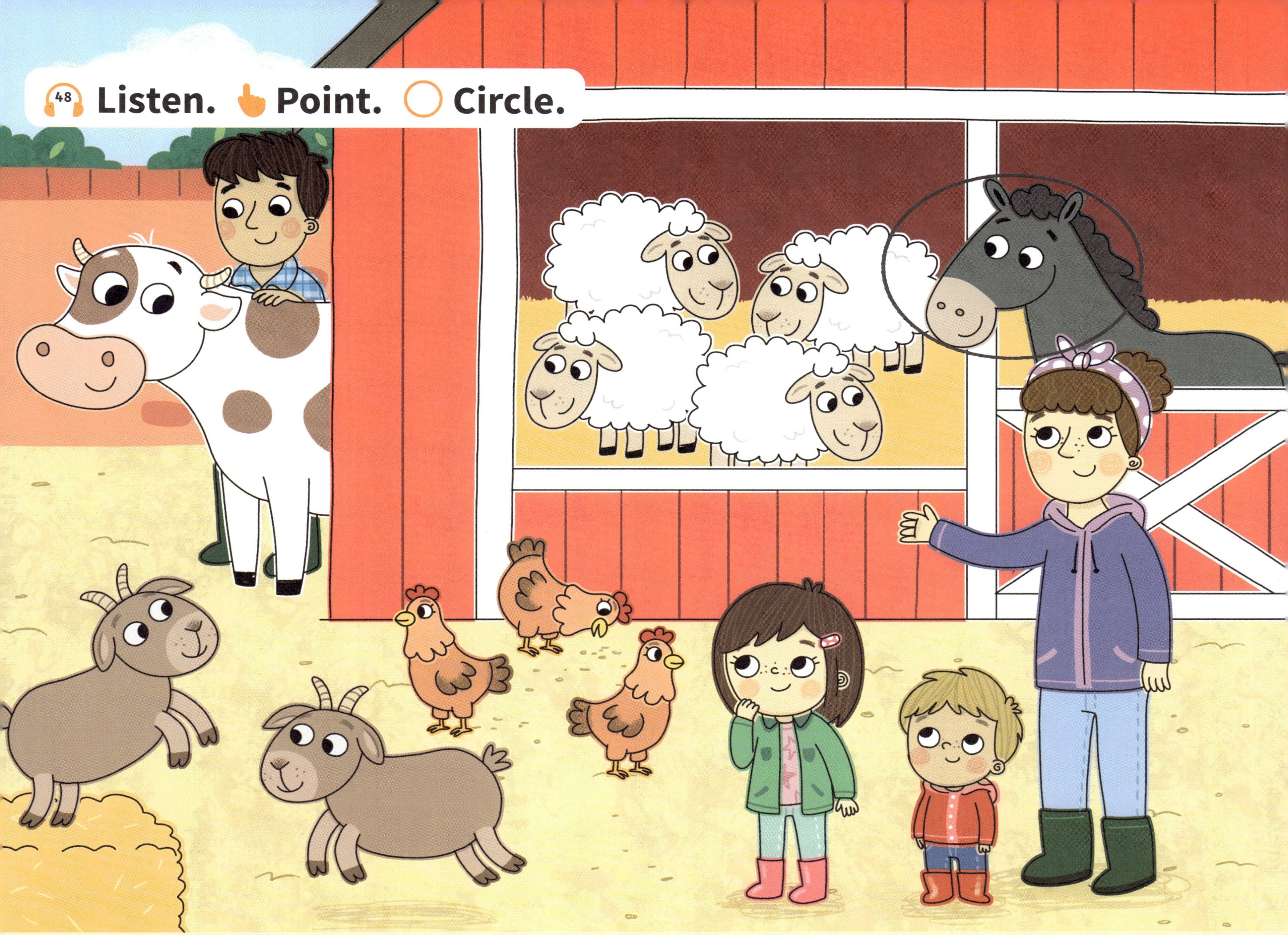

Listen. Follow. Stick. Say.

6 **Language practice:** *It's a (horse / sheep / chicken / cow / goat). It's got (a long neck / four legs / small ears).*

50 🎧 **Listen.** ⭕ **Trace.** ✏️ **Colour.** 💬 **Say.**

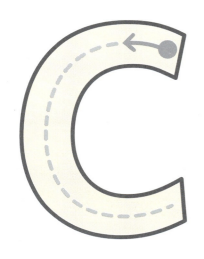

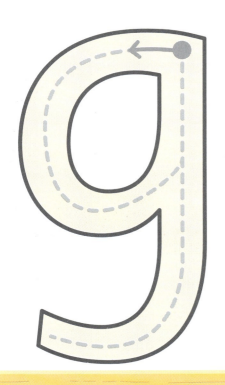

▶ 🎧 51 **Listen.** **Stubborn goats!**

1

2

3

4

▶️ 🎧 52 Listen. 👆 Point. ⭕ Circle.

6 Language presentation: *A (horse) can / can't (jump / swim / fly / walk / run).*

Listen. 🖊 **Colour.** 🎵 **Sing.**

✋ **Count.** ◯ **Circle.** 🟧 **Say.**

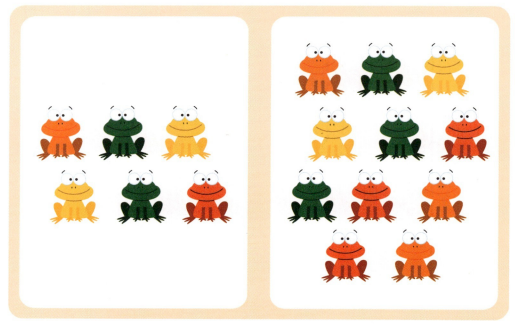

Look. Match.

 **Listen.** **Draw.** **Say.**

6 *It's a (horse / sheep / chicken / cow / goat). It's got (a long neck / four legs / small ears).*

Look. Make. Say.

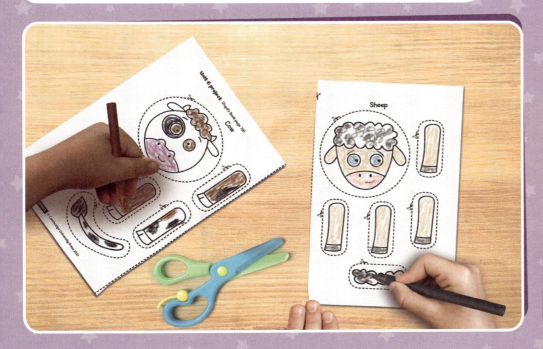

55 🎧 **Listen.** 🔍 **Find.** ⭕ **Circle.** 💬 **Say.**

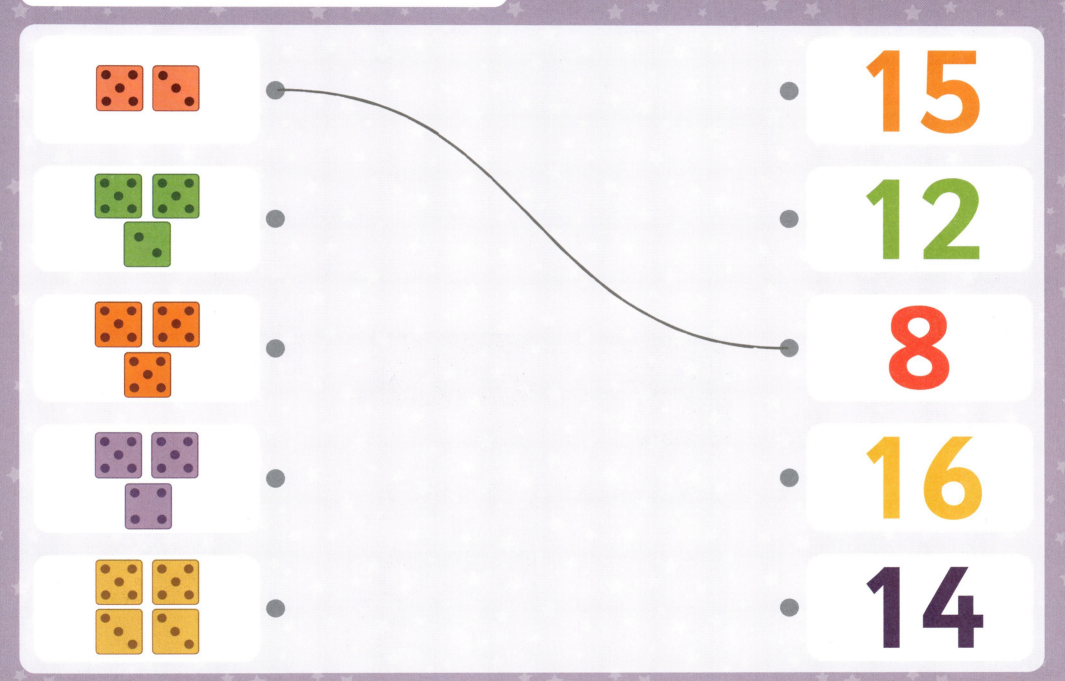

7 My favourite food

 56 **Listen to the song.**

57 🎧 Listen. 👆 Point. ⭕ Circle.

🎧 58 **Listen.** 🟠 **Stick.** ⭕ **Trace.** 🟧 **Say.**

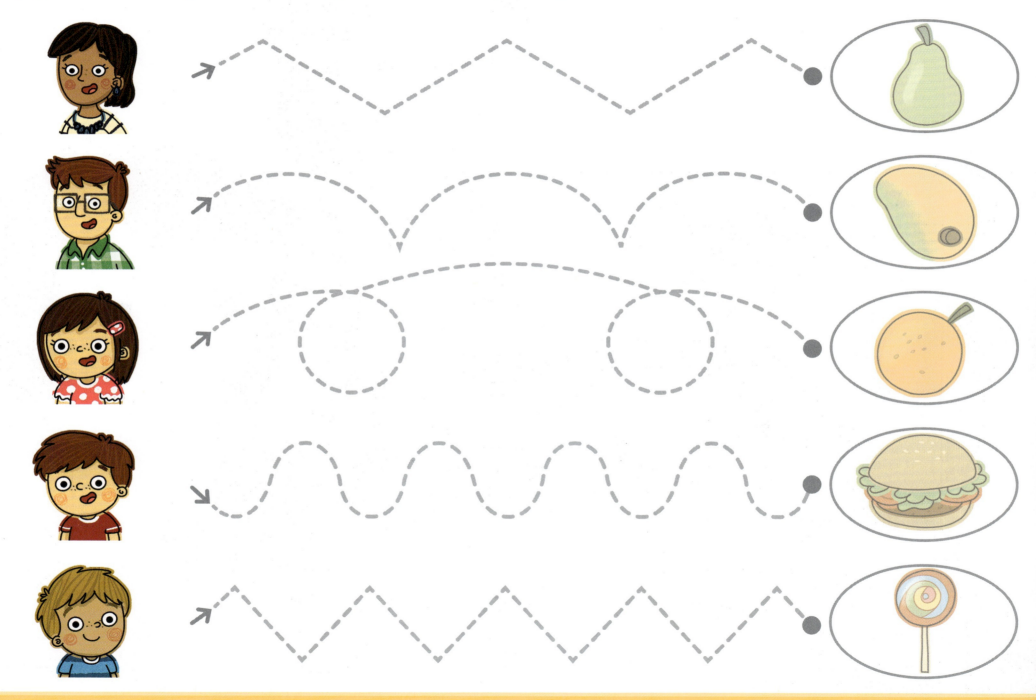

7 Language practice: *Can I have (a mango / an orange / a pear / a burger / a lolly), please?*

59 🎧 **Listen.** ⭕ **Trace.** ✏️ **Colour.** 💬 **Say.**

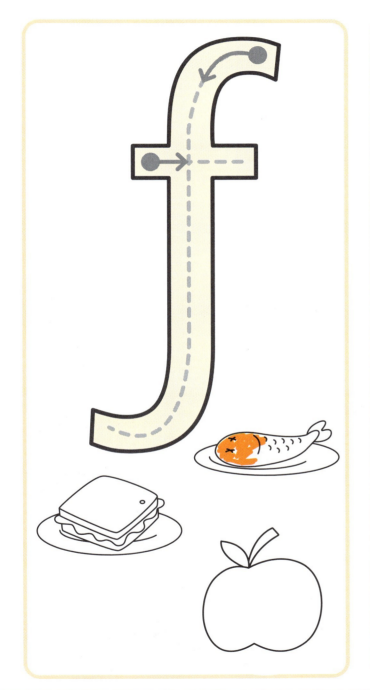

 ▶ 🎧 60 **Listen.** **Pea soup**

1

2

3

4

7 Language presentation: *Do you like (eggs / fish / chips / bread / cheese)? Yes, I do. / No, I don't.*

Listen. **Draw.** **Sing.**

🎧 63 **Listen.** ⭕ **Trace.** ✋ **Count.** ⭕ **Circle.**

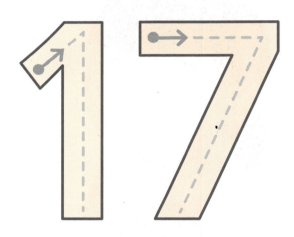

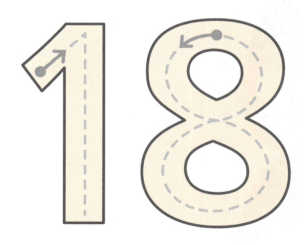

👁 Look. 🃏 Match.

🎧 64 Listen. ⭕ Circle. 💬 Say.

7 *Do you like (eggs / fish / chips / bread / cheese / mangoes / oranges / pears / burgers / lollies)? Yes, I do. / No, I don't.*

Look. Make. Say.

8 My senses

8 **Unit topic introduction:** The five senses

🎧 66 Listen. 👆 Point. ⭕ Circle.

 Listen. Stick. Match. Say.

8 **Language practice:** *Can you (feel / hear / taste / see / smell) (the rain)? Yes, I can. / No, I can't.*

68 Listen. ◯ Trace. ✏ Colour. 💬 Say.

Listen. A wonderful day

1

2

3

4

5

6

7

8

▶ 🎧 70 **Listen.** 👆 **Point.** ◯ **Circle.**

8 **Language presentation:** *What can you (see / smell / taste / hear / feel)? I can (see) (a leaf / grass / watermelon / lemon / a bee).*

Listen. ○ **Circle.** ♫ **Sing.**

👁 **Look.** ✏️ **Draw.** 🖍 **Colour.**

👁 Look. 📙 Match.

👁 Look. ✏ Colour. 💬 Say.

Look. Make. Say.

9 Holidays!

🎧 Listen. ⬭ Stick. 📙 Match. 💬 Say.

9 **Language practice:** *beach, sea; How many (boats / kites / shells) can you see? I can see (four) (boats).*

75 🎧 **Listen.** ⭕ **Trace.** ✏️ **Colour.** 💬 **Say.**

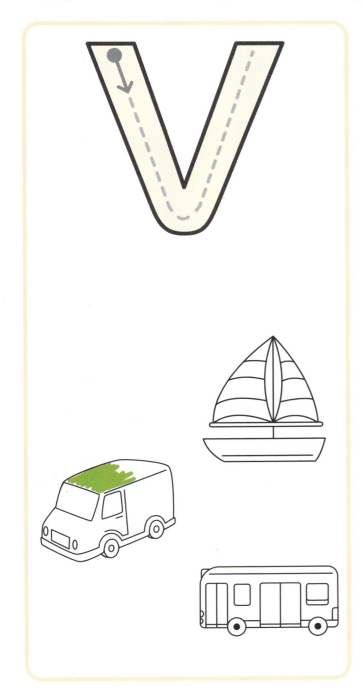

▶ 🎧 76 **Listen.** **You can do it, Sam!**

1

2

3

4

9 **Language presentation:** *I'm (making sandcastles / playing with shells / eating ice cream / drinking lemonade / swimming / taking photos).*

 **Listen.** ⭕ **Trace.** ✋ **Count.** ⭕ **Circle.**

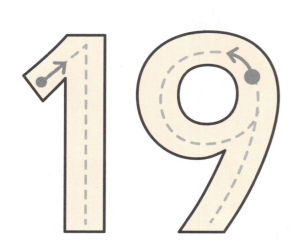

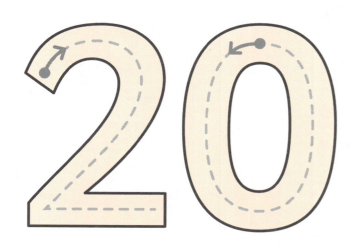

 Look. Match.

🎧 **Listen.** ➡➡ **Follow.** ✏ **Colour.** 💬 **Say.**

9 *I'm (making sandcastles / playing with shells / eating ice cream / drinking lemonade / swimming / taking photos).*

Look. Make. Say.

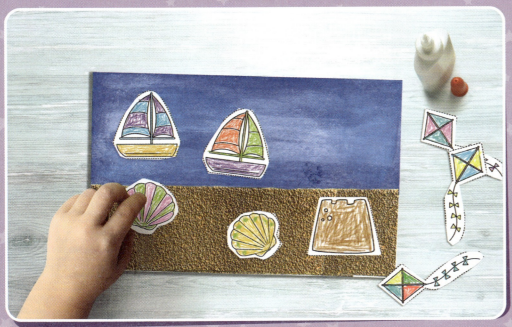

👁 Look. ✋ Count. ✏️ Colour.

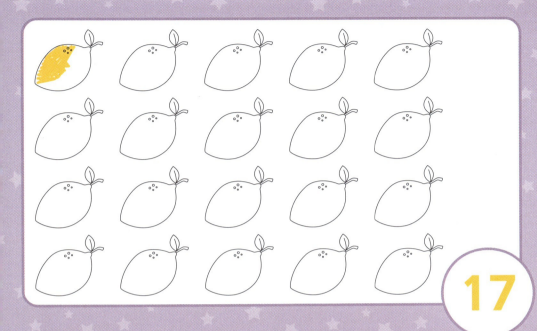

17

18

19

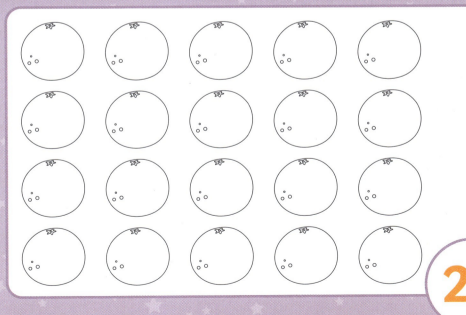

20

Thanks and Acknowledgements

Authors' thanks

Many thanks to everyone at Cambridge University Press for their dedication and hard work in extraordinarily complicated circumstances, and in particular to:

Liane Grainger for her unwavering professionalism and her irrepressible joviality;

Emily Hird for her endless enthusiasm, good humour and sound judgement;

Jane Holt for her unflagging energy and her ability to bring the whole, sprawling project together;

Vanessa Gold for her hard work and sound editorial contribution.

Catherine Ball, Stephanie Howard and Carolyn Wright for their hard work helping to review, correct and knead the manuscript into shape.

Our thoughts and hearts go out to all the teachers and their pupils who have suffered and continue to suffer the devastating effects of the global pandemic that has changed all our lives. Stay strong.

Dedications

For my lovely sisters, Elaine and Teresa, with much love. – CN

For Paloma, Pablo and Carlota, keep on smiling, love – MT

Caroline Nixon and Michael Tomlinson, Murcia, Spain

The publishers and authors would like to thank the following contributors:

Additional writing by Lesley Koustaff, Susan Rivers and Catherine Ball.

Book design and page make-up by Blooberry Design.

Cover design by Blooberry Design.

Commissioned photography by Blooberry Design.

Freelance editing by Catherine Ball, Stephanie Howard and Carolyn Wright.

Audio recording and production by Ian Harker.

Original songs and chants by Robert Lee.

Songs and chants production by Jake Carter.

Animation production by QBS and Collaborate Agency.

The authors and publishers acknowledge the following sources of copyright material and are grateful for the permissions granted. While every effort has been made, it has not always been possible to identify the sources of all the material used, or to trace all copyright holders. If any omissions are brought to our notice, we will be happy to include the appropriate acknowledgements on reprinting and in the next update to the digital edition, as applicable.

Key: U = Unit.

Photography

These photos are sourced from Getty Images.

U0: antadi1332/iStock/Getty Images Plus; **U1:** Eclipse_images/E+; Jessica Peterson; Maskot; Supawat Punnanon/EyeEm; Vicnt/iStock/Getty Images Plus; Athiwat Poolsawad/EyeEm; Kukiat Boontung/EyeEm; Dontstop/iStock/Getty Images Plus; Picsfive/iStock/Getty Images Plus; Photochecker/iStock/Getty Images Plus; Strixcode/iStock/Getty Images Plus; Irina_Strelnikova/iStock/Getty Images Plus; Asya_mix/iStock/Getty Images Plus; Lubushka/iStock/Getty Images Plus; Mai Vu/iStock/Getty Images Plus; antadi1332/iStock/Getty Images Plus; **U2:** FangXiaNuo/E+; Jack Hollingsworth/Photodisc; kali9/E+; Indeed; Welcome to buy my photos/Moment; FangXiaNuo/iStock/Getty Images Plus; Flavia Morlachetti/Moment; Bruce Laurance; ajr_images/iStock/Getty Images Plus; Fancy/Veer/Corbis/Getty Images Plus; Jose Luis Pelaez Inc/DigitalVision; Johner Images; Karen Moskowitz/Stockbyte; Adie Bush/Cultura; Irina_Strelnikova/iStock/Getty Images Plus; Asya_mix/iStock/Getty Images Plus; Lubushka/iStock/Getty Images Plus; Mai Vu/iStock/Getty Images Plus; antadi1332/iStock/Getty Images Plus; **U3:** Andy Crawford; Zing Images/The Image Bank/Getty Images Plus; ViewStock; KatarzynaBialasiewicz/iStock/Getty Images Plus; Jacek Kadaj/Moment; John Keeble/Moment; Martin Deja/Moment; Jon Lovette/DigitalVision; Yasin Emir Akbas/iStock/Getty Images Plus; Chakrapong Worathat/EyeEm; Pepifoto/E+; Chillim/iStock/Getty Images Plus; Eugenesergeev/iStock/Getty Images Plus; Irina_Strelnikova/iStock/Getty Images Plus; Asya_mix/iStock/Getty Images Plus; Lubushka/iStock/Getty Images Plus; Mai Vu/iStock/Getty Images Plus; antadi1332/iStock/Getty Images Plus; **U4:** Buck Forester/Moment; Maskot; JW LTD/Stone; Irina_Strelnikova/iStock/Getty Images Plus; Asya_mix/iStock/Getty Images Plus; Lubushka/iStock/Getty Images Plus; Mai Vu/iStock/Getty Images Plus; antadi1332/iStock/Getty Images Plus; **U5:** RgStudio/E+; Sally Anscombe/Stone; Wundervisuals/E+; gui00878/E+; MsMoloko/iStock/Getty Images Plus; R A Kearton/Moment; **U6:** Andreas Häuslbetz/iStock/Getty Images Plus; Peter Cade/Stone; Bluefootage/The Image Bank/Getty Images Plus; Robert Llewellyn/Corbis; Digital Zoo/Photodisc; narvikk/E+; GlobalP/iStock/Getty Images Plus; Samantha French/EyeEm; bobtphoto/E+; Ljupco/iStock/Getty Images Plus; Lew Robertson/Stone; Irina_Strelnikova/iStock/Getty Images Plus; **U7:** Chris Mellor/Lonely Planet Images/Getty Images Plus; Jose Luis Pelaez Inc/DigitalVision; wundervisuals/E+; Inacio Pires/EyeEm; Yuji Sakai/DigitalVision; VLIET/E+; Franckreporter/E+; Pixelprof/iStock/Getty Images Plus; Henry Arden/Cultura; Creativ Studio Heinemann; Lartal/Photolibrary/Getty Images Plus; Maximilian Stock Ltd/Photolibrary/Getty Images Plus; Joff Lee/The Image Bank; Suparat Malipoom/EyeEm; Irina_Strelnikova/iStock/Getty Images Plus; Asya_mix/iStock/Getty Images Plus; Lubushka/iStock/Getty Images Plus; Mai Vu/iStock/Getty Images Plus; antadi1332/iStock/Getty Images Plus; **U8:** PeopleImages/E+; Jose Luis Pelaez Inc/DigitalVision; Richard Jacobson/EyeEm; RuslanDashinsky/E+; mielag/iStock/Getty Images Plus; andy_Q/iStock/Getty Images Plus; Graham Swain/EyeEm; Jade Brookbank/Image Source; Paula French/EyeEm; Manolo guijarro/Moment; Henry Arden/Cultura; 2A Images; Irina_Strelnikova/iStock/Getty Images Plus; Asya_mix/iStock/Getty Images Plus; Lubushka/iStock/Getty Images Plus; Mai Vu/iStock/Getty Images Plus; antadi1332/iStock/Getty Images Plus; **U9:** Kathy Collins/Photographer's Choice/Getty Images Plus; Allan Baxter/Photodisc; Geri Lavrov/Moment Open; Maciej Nicgorski/EyeEm; PM Images/Stone; s-cphoto/E+; Floortje/E+; Gaffera/E+; Peter Dazeley/The Image Bank; Irina_Strelnikova/iStock/Getty Images Plus; Photographer/iStock/Getty Images Plus; to_csa/E+; Asya_mix/iStock/Getty Images Plus; Lubushka/iStock/Getty Images Plus; Mai Vu/iStock/Getty Images Plus; antadi1332/iStock/Getty Images Plus.

The following images are sourced from other Libraries

U2: Oleg Beloborodov/Alamy Stock Photo; U4: RTimages/Alamy Stock Photo; U6:SpeedKingz/Shutterstock; U8: Silatip/Shutterstock.

Illustrations

Amy Zhing; Beatriz Castro; Begoña Corbalan; Dean Gray; Louise Forshaw and Collaborate Agency artists

Cover illustration by Collaborate Agency.